THE BLESSING OF COMMITMENT

Study Guide & Journal
for Releasing Wealth &
Riches into Your Life

Bobby Hilton

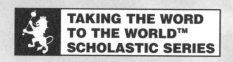

TAKING THE WORD TO THE WORLD™ SCHOLASTIC SERIES

ISBN 1-930766-38-6

Bishop Bobby Hilton Ministries, Inc.
690 Northland Blvd.
Forest Park, OH 45240
(513) 851-WORD (9673) • Fax: (513) 742-3458
Website: www.bobbyhilton.org

Compiler and Editor: June Ridgway, M.S.W., Ed.D.
Copy Editor: LaVerne Summerlin, Professor of English, University of Cincinnati
Cover Design: Vernard Fields, graFICs design for FIC Music
Interior Design & Production: Cathie Tibbetts, CAT Graphics
Photography: © 2004 by Hanan Isachar

This Book Belongs to

TO: Elsie
_____

Bobby Hull

Date Started
_____

Date Completed
_____

TABLE OF CONTENTS

HOW TO USE
THIS BOOK

The *Taking the Word to the World™ Scholastic Series* is designed to help you apply the biblical principles presented in my books, audiotapes, and videotapes to your personal life. The study guides, journals, and other educational materials in the series are structured to promote positive change that is rooted in spiritual growth.

This study guide and journal offers an in-depth study of the topics that were presented in *The Blessing of Commitment: Releasing Wealth & Riches Into Your Life.* My first objective is to enhance your knowledge of Scripture and encourage you to delve deeper into the biblical principles presented in the book. Second, I want to help you attain higher levels of spiritual awareness and consciousness. This is accomplished, in part, through your journal writing. Ultimately, the purpose of this book is to help you *renew your mind* so you can connect to the Light of the Creator, which releases wealth and riches into your life.

Each chapter contains the following elements.

Foundational Scripture illustrates the predominant spiritual principles and message presented in the chapter.

Chapter Summary summarizes the chapter's essential themes.

Study Questions reinforce the biblical principles and related information covered in the chapter. This section also gives you an opportunity to conduct further research using the Bible, commentaries, and other resources to complete your answers.

Meditation offers a key concept to be internalized for spiritual growth. The meditation is designed to open your mind so that the deeper meaning of the teachings will penetrate your spirit.

Reflections provide questions for self-assessment and spiritual correction in a journal format. This section helps you look within yourself to identify internal blockages that hinder your spiritual growth, and it provides insight into how you can eliminate them from your life.

God's Path for You helps you identify your correct spiritual path, particularly when the way may not be clear. As you journal your thoughts, the path God has for you is illuminated, keeping you on course to your destination.

Group Discussion Questions generate lively discussion for classroom settings and study groups. The group discussion questions build upon the themes covered in the independent study and journal writing sections.

Quote from the Bishop offers words of encouragement as you prepare for the *blessing of commitment.*

At the end of the book, chapter study questions are provided in a **test format**. Tear out pages 163–172 along the perforation to use as a final test. This test can also be downloaded from my website: www.bobbyhilton.org. Completed tests can be faxed to (513) 742-3458 or mailed to:

> BBHM
> 690 Northland Blvd.
> Forest Park, OH 45240
> ATTN: Publications Department.

Please retain a copy of your test for your records. We will grade your test and mail your score to you. **Certificates of Completion** will be issued to individuals who have a correct score of 70% to 100% on the test.

Research Projects and a **Scripture Index** for quick reference can also be found at the end of the book.

These tools have been made available to help you on your spiritual journey. As you progress in your spiritual work and make positive changes, you will experience a *renewing of your mind.* God's perfect will for you shall unfold, and *wealth and riches shall be released into your life.*

Because of Him, I am
Bishop Bobby Hilton, Ph.D.

TEACHERS AND GROUP LEADERS

If you want to use this book for group study, I suggest the following:

1. Prayerfully commit the study to the LORD and seek His guidance in every step. Choose someone who will diligently prepare to lead the group.

2. Have each student purchase *The Blessing of Commitment: Releasing Wealth and Riches into Your Life* along with this guide. Encourage your students to do the study questions and journal sections at home week by week. Each week will require an average of one to two hours of study, depending on the topics presented in the chapter.

3. Discuss—when you meet as a group—the study questions first. Then proceed with the group discussion questions.

4. Have students complete the research projects by the end of the course.

To obtain the answer key to the study questions or for additional information, write, call or e-mail:

BBHM
690 Northland Blvd.
Forest Park, Ohio 45240
(513) 851-(WORD) 9673
scholasticseries@bobbyhilton.org

CHAPTER 1

IT'S TIME FOR A CHANGE

*Do not be conformed to this world (this age), [fashioned after and adapted to its external, superficial customs], but be **transformed** (changed) by the [entire] renewal of your mind [by its new ideals and its new attitude], so that you may prove [for yourselves] what is the good and acceptable and perfect will of God, even the thing which is good and acceptable and perfect [in His sight for you].*

(Romans 12:2, The Amplified Bible)

Chapter Summary

There is a divine blessing over the lives of believers who totally commit to God. Scripture declares that if we follow His instructions and live according to His Word, God will release wealth and riches into our lives (Psalm 112:1–3).

Unfortunately, due to traditional doctrine and lack of knowledge, many Christians have a mind-set that makes it difficult for them to receive God's Word concerning prosperity.

You cannot allow your mind to be bound (conformed) to tradition or to the limits of our physical world. You must seek higher levels of consciousness and spirituality so you can receive His Word. The LORD is faithful and shall fulfill the promise. *Wealth and riches will be released into your life!*

Study Questions

1. Using three Scripture references, explain the meaning of "transformed by the renewing of our minds."

2. What factors have contributed to the acceptance of debt as a "part of life" in today's culture?

3. When the children of Israel left Egypt, they had doubts about God's willingness to fulfill His promises. What caused this doubt? Were they able to overcome it?

4. Why does the LORD deliver His people from debt?

5. True or False: Money is the root of all evil.

6. Deuteronomy, chapter 28, describes the blessings God has for His people. List five blessings noted in this chapter. What must one do to receive these blessings?

7. How does one move from confessing God's promises that have been declared in the spirit realm, to manifestation in the physical realm?

8. What is God's plan concerning the wealth of the sinner?

9. Hosea 4:6 says, "My people are destroyed for lack of knowledge." What is God's position towards those who reject knowledge?

10. Isaiah 10:27 tells us, "...and the yoke shall be destroyed because of the anointing." Explain how this aspect of the anointing applies to the burden of debt.

Meditation

Wealth and riches are in God's Kingdom and it is time for me to possess them. But, I must first have a commitment to God. I cannot accept one part of the Word and reject the other. I must do that which is pleasing to Him, and His will shall come forth in my life.

Reflections

Most Christians understand that it is God's will to heal our bodies and save our loved ones. But the Word of God also tells us that the Lord will make us rich (Proverbs 10:22). From a spiritual perspective, explain the meaning of being *rich*. Do you think of yourself as rich? Below, write your answer.

God's Path for You

The Bible tells us that the wealth and riches of the sinner belong to the righteous, for whom it was laid up (Proverbs 13:22). It also tells us not to worry or be envious when sinners prosper more quickly than the righteous (Psalm 37:1, 7).

Resting in the LORD, and waiting patiently for Him is not always easy. Do you ever find yourself becoming impatient or anxious about God's plan to release wealth and riches into your life? What do you do to strengthen your faith in God's timing? Below, write your answer.

_____

_____

_____

_____

_____

_____

_____

_____

_____

_____

_____

_____

_____

Group Discussion

1. Romans 12:2 states that believers should not conform to this world, but be transformed by the renewing of our minds. What do you think contributes to many believers conforming to the world's way of living rather than living according to the Word of God?

2. Why has it been difficult for some Christians to believe they are destined to prosper? What can be done to change this mind-set?

3. What can the body of Christ do to prepare for the transfer of wealth described in Proverbs 13:22?

Quote from the Bishop...

The Lord gives us power to get wealth
(Deuteronomy 8:18) and when He blesses
us it is for His glory and purpose.
Christians must be liberated from
the mind-set of "not enough" and
"just enough." We serve the God of
much more than enough (El Shaddai).

CHAPTER 2

CAN YOU STAND TO BE BLESSED?

If ye be willing and obedient,
ye shall eat the good
of the land .

(Isaiah 1:19)

Chapter Summary

God is looking for people who are willing to obey Him and respect Him for who He is. The Word of God tells us that the riches of the land are ours, but we must be in right relationship with Him to receive them.

In this chapter, you read how God increased His people in prosperity and power, but they did not know what to do with it (Hosea 4:7). This is why I pose the question, *"Can you stand to be blessed?"*

The prophet warned God's people not to serve other gods when they increased in prosperity. This is a sin against Him. The LORD will rain down *the blessing of commitment and release wealth and riches*, but this blessing is going to be released on those who know what to do with it!

Study Questions

1. Why are some people afraid of money?

2. What are God's instructions for people who borrow from their tithes (Leviticus 27:31)?

3. How does the Bible describe someone who does not pay his or her tithes and offerings? What are the consequences for disobeying God's instructions concerning this matter?

4. Blessings are a testimony of God's _____.

5. It is our Father's good _____ to give us the
   _____ (Luke 12:32).

6. If you remain thankful and pay your vows unto the
   Most High, in the day of trouble you can call upon Him
   and He will _____ you.

Meditation

The spirit of debt should not be in my home. The Word of
God declares that His people shall prosper and have good
success (Joshua 1:8).

The *anointing* releases the yoke of debt. I reach into my soul
to connect to the anointing that removes all burdens and
destroys all yokes (Isaiah 10:27).

Reflections

Financial problems are all too common among believers. Yet, the Word of God says that if we are willing and obedient, we shall eat the best from the land. Why is it difficult for some believers to obtain victory in this area while others seem to prosper with ease? Below, write your thoughts.

_____

_____

_____

_____

_____

_____

_____

_____

_____

_____

_____

_____

_____

_____

_____

_____

God's Path for You

God must be able to trust you with the tithe. You cannot say, "God when You send me $60,000, then I'll give my tithe." If you only have $6.00 give Him 60¢!

Do you tithe? Write below the reasons you do or do not tithe. Describe the impact your position on tithing has had on your life. Substantiate your thoughts with Scripture citations.

_____

_____

_____

_____

_____

_____

_____

_____

_____

_____

_____

_____

_____

_____

_____

Group Discussion

1. What is the purpose of tithing? Do you believe the instructions for tithing given in Leviticus 27:30–31 are relevant today? What instructions are offered in the New Testament concerning tithing?

2. Why is it difficult for some people to remain balanced when God blesses them?

Quote from the Bishop...

God has a purpose for blessing
those who are committed to Him.
He prospers us to finance His Kingdom.
When God finds trustworthy people,
He blesses them even more.

CHAPTER 3

TOTAL DELIVERANCE

*If the Son therefore shall
make you free,
ye shall be free indeed.*

(John 8:36)

Chapter Summary

Regardless of what is happening in your life, you can receive *total deliverance*. Jesus said, "The Spirit of the Lord is upon me, ...to preach deliverance to the captives, ...and to set at liberty them that are bruised (Luke 4:18). Our Lord and Savior came to set us free from the bondage of sin, allowing the Holy Spirit to dwell and empower our lives.

Everything God does for you is for His glory. He will deliver you from the strongholds of addiction to give Himself glory. The God we serve will release wealth and riches into your life so that He may be glorified. When you are blessed, His glory is revealed.

Study Questions

1. Explain the meaning of *deliverance*.

2. List five tools the enemy uses to keep people in bondage.

3. True or False: Confession is an essential step for obtaining deliverance.

4. In the fight against the enemy, what are three weapons believers should possess and use?

5. In Genesis 12:2–3, what did God promise Abram (Abraham)?

6. Explain justification through faith.

7. When Abraham left Egypt, he was very rich in cattle, silver, and gold. How did he accumulate these possessions?

Meditation

God wants a delivered body of believers; people who have a testimony of who He is. As my Deliverer, Fire Baptizer, Holy Ghost-Filler, and Sanctifier, He never changes. He is the same yesterday, today, and forever (Hebrews 13:8). Everything I need to obtain victory can be found in Him.

Reflections

To one degree or another, we all have been prisoners to our self-centered egos and selfish desires. We battle with negative impulses from within that are often powerful and ultimately self-destructive. Is there an aspect of your nature that needs to change? What difficulties does it present in your life? What are you doing to make the positive changes and corrections that need to occur from within? Give each of these questions careful thought; then write your insights below.

_____

_____

_____

_____

_____

_____

_____

_____

_____

_____

_____

_____

_____

_____

God's Path for You

All of us have been delivered from something and we thank God for it. Take a few moments to reflect on an area of your life in which you have experienced total deliverance. Below, write your testimony.

_____

_____

_____

_____

_____

_____

_____

_____

_____

_____

_____

_____

_____

_____

_____

_____

Group Discussion

1. Read Genesis 12:1–3, Genesis 28:14 and Galatians 3:3–29. What does the Bible mean when it speaks of the blessing of Abraham?

2. Who is Abraham's seed? Explain.

Quote from the Bishop...

Genuine freedom
is from the bondage
that occurs within.

CHAPTER 4

MUCH MORE
THAN ENOUGH

And they spake unto Moses, saying,
The people bring much more
than enough for the service
of the work, which the
LORD commanded to make.

(Exodus 36:5)

Chapter Summary

When the LORD saved you, it was not His intention for you to be saved, yet live in lack. When He delivered you, He did not intend for you to just barely make ends meet. For some of you, it looks like you're so low and so far behind financially; you can't see yourself *coming out.* Just remember: God made everything that is glorious and valuable for His people. When you operate according to His principles, you can expect an increase. Your harvest will come.

To experience the dimension of *much more than enough,* you must arm yourself spiritually. You must place yourself in a position where God can use you for His purpose and glory. Then the LORD will release blessings, allowing you to live in prosperity, and finance His Kingdom.

Study Questions

1. How long were the children of Israel held in bondage by the Egyptians:

   a) 200 years b) 300 years c) over 400 years

2. The wealth of the sinner is laid up for the _____.

3. After giving the children of Israel wealth and freeing them from the Egyptians, what did God ask of them?

4. Explain God's principle of increase.

5. At the beginning of the Book of Exodus, the children of Israel were slaves and had nothing. In Exodus 36:5, they have *much more than enough* to do God's work. Spiritually, how did this dramatic change come about?

Meditation

The Word of God says, "But the people that do know their God shall be strong, and do exploits" (Daniel 11:32b). Exploits are exceedingly mighty things. I will believe in the Name of the LORD and put my trust in Him; and He shall empower me to do exceedingly mighty and great things.

Reflections

People who *know* God are empowered to do great things. Think about an "exploit" you were able to perform, only because the power of God was working through you. Below, describe your experience.

_____

_____

_____

_____

_____

_____

_____

_____

_____

_____

_____

_____

_____

_____

_____

God's Path for You

Those who sow seed sparingly into the Kingdom of God will reap sparingly. Whoever sows generously will reap generously. How would you describe your level of sowing into the Kingdom? What are your goals concerning financing the Kingdom? Below, write your answer.

Group Discussion

1. Why are many church leaders afraid to teach about prosperity?

2. List five criteria that can be used to determine the wisdom of investing one's time, talents, and finances to a particular church or ministry.

Quote from the Bishop...

God gives seed to the sower.
If He sees you being a sower,
He will give you more seed to sow
(1 Corinthians 9:10). The manifestation
of every promise of God's Word can come
forth in your life. It's all for His glory.
God is canceling debt and going to cancel
even more debt so that you can tell
the world "God did it!" You'll be blessed with
much more than enough.

CHAPTER 5

DETERMINED TO PRAISE

*PRAISE ye the LORD. Blessed is
the man that feareth the LORD,
that delighteth greatly in
his commandments.*

*His seed shall be mighty
upon earth: the generation
of the upright shall be blessed.*

*Wealth and riches shall be
in his house: and his
righteousness endureth for ever.*

(Psalm 112:1–3)

Chapter Summary

Being able to praise the Lord at all times is a level of spirituality that every believer should strive to attain. You may not always be able to praise God based on what you see. Many times you have to praise Him because of His Word. Your money might be funny. You may be talked about and lied on. You might have some trouble. But continue to praise God for what His Word says.

The Word of God tells us there is an end to our trials (Proverbs 23:18). Therefore, it doesn't matter how long you've been in pain, or how long you have been crying, because surely there is an end. Your expectation will not be cut off. Wealth and riches shall be in your house!

Study Questions

1. What was the adversary trying to prove to God about Job?

2. The Psalms written by King David often tell of praising the LORD regardless of the circumstances. Find three Psalms that reflect a posture of praise to the Creator at all times. What conclusion does David reach in each of these Psalms?

3. Describe two aspects of our inner being that ignite a release of wealth and riches into our lives (Psalm 112).

Meditation

My greatest desire is to be in proper relationship with God. My life shall show forth His praise (Isaiah 43:21). The purpose for which I was created shall be fulfilled.

Reflections

Our greatest joy and fulfillment comes when the Light of the Creator is able to flow freely through our lives. As you embrace spiritual growth and true transformation, you will not only be blessed; you'll be a blessing. Is there anything within your inner being that short circuits God's Light from flowing freely through you? Below, write your insights.

_____

_____

_____

_____

_____

_____

_____

_____

_____

_____

_____

_____

_____

_____

_____

God's Path for You

Have you ever had a *pass the test* experience? Did you utilize the power of praise during this time? How was your life transformed? Below, write about this experience.

_____

_____

_____

_____

_____

_____

_____

_____

_____

_____

_____

_____

_____

_____

_____

_____

_____

_____

_____

Group Discussion

1. Many people are wandering aimlessly through life without a sense of purpose or meaning. How would you minister to someone who has this outlook on life?

2. Meditating on the Word of God and praising Him are "spiritual tools" that enable us to connect to Him and fulfill His purpose. What other spiritual tools has God provided so that His will is accomplished in the earth?

Quote from the Bishop...

When we praise God, His Light is revealed.
Pain, chaos, and suffering are replaced
with joy, fulfillment, and bliss.
It is through people who are
determined to praise that the
world will see the glory of God.

CHAPTER 6

GET IN POSITION

*And it shall come to pass, if thou shalt
hearken diligently unto the voice of the
LORD thy God, to observe and to do all
his commandments which I command thee
this day, that the LORD thy God will set thee
on high above all nations of the earth:*

*And all these blessings shall come on thee,
and overtake thee, if thou shalt hearken
unto the voice of the LORD thy God.*

(Deuteronomy 28:1–2)

Chapter Summary

We learned about the blessings God has for us in Deuteronomy 28:1–13. When you commit to God, He commands the blessing. All you need to do is position yourself to receive them.

Wealth and riches are part of the salvation package. When you gave your life to Christ and received the baptism of the Holy Ghost, you positioned yourself to receive from the Spirit of God. When you get God, you get all that He is, and everything for which He stands.

Study Questions

1. True or False: Holiness refers to a denomination.

2. True or False: A lifestyle of transgression is easier than a lifestyle of holiness.

3. Explain, using the principles discussed in this chapter, the meaning of being *humble*.

4. Why did God bless Abraham?

5. Citing the New Testament, find an example of God freeing His people from debt.

6. True or False: One can know God without knowing His Word.

7. John 6:63 says, "It is the spirit that quickeneth; the flesh profiteth nothing...." Explain the meaning of this verse.

Meditation

As I commit to God, my soul is cleansed. I am transformed and become what God has called me to be. When the world can see Jesus through my life, I can expect blessings to come. I have positioned myself to be blessed.

Reflections

Are you in position to receive from the Lord? Honestly reflecting on the following questions can help you pinpoint the areas you need to work on to *get in position*.

- Am I living holy?
- Do I faithfully give my tithes and offerings?
- Am I determined to praise Him regardless of the circumstances?
- Have I made a commitment to studying and knowing the Word of God?

In the space below, write your answers.

_____

_____

_____

_____

_____

_____

_____

_____

_____

_____

_____

_____

God's Path for You

This chapter discusses having a strong Scriptural foundation in the Word of God. Many times people rush out to do a work for the Lord without a foundation. But if you don't have a foundation, you cannot stand.

Have you ever rushed to do something for the Lord and later discovered that it was not the right thing to do? How could this mistake have been avoided? Below, describe your experience.

_____

_____

_____

_____

_____

_____

_____

_____

_____

_____

_____

_____

_____

_____

_____

Group Discussion

1. There are various opinions on what constitutes a lifestyle of holiness. What do you think are the essentials of a holy life? Why is this lifestyle sometimes considered undesirable? How have church people contributed to perpetuating the myth that a holy life an undesirable life?

2. Many people are motivated to seek the LORD because they desire money, houses, and other material things. What usually happens in these situations? What can we do to make sure that material gain is not the focus of our relationship with the LORD?

Quote from the bishop...

You should not come to the altar
just because the Word of God says
He will give you power to get wealth.
You should not get on your knees just
because you want the Lord to bless you
with more money. You already know
the Word of God says that the
blessing of the Lord makes you rich.
It's going to happen because you are
positioning yourself to glorify Him.

CHAPTER 7

THE WORD IN US

*Thy word have I hid
in mine heart,
that I might not
sin against thee.*

(Psalm 119:11)

Chapter Summary

Psalm 119:11 notes the importance of saturating ourselves with the Word and planting it within our hearts. Joshua 1:8 encourages us to go to the extent of meditating on God's Word day and night, until it flows out of our mouths.

Why would one need to engage in such intensive study of the Word of God? Because it helps us achieve victory. When difficulties arise, you'll have a Word inside reminding you that you don't have to accept the disappointments. You'll know what the Word of God has promised, and consequently, remain committed regardless of the circumstances. The Word in you provides a hedge against the enemy and protects your deliverance.

Study Questions

1. Using practical, real life examples, explain the difference between knowledge and wisdom.

2. True or False: Joy is derived from external circumstances and situations.

3. True or False: God gives wisdom only to people who are spiritually mature.

4. Explain, using at least three Scripture references, the biblical meaning of *faith*.

Meditation

I will keep God's Word deep within my heart. His Word purifies my soul. Jesus Himself sanctifies and cleanses me with the washing of water by the Word (Eph. 5:26).

Reflections

Studying God's Word and planting it deep within our souls should be a high priority for every believer. Unfortunately, the demands of the world can distract us from setting aside sufficient time to study. How much time do you devote to studying God's Word? Do you feel it is enough? What changes or adjustments can you make that will allow you to spend more time studying His Word? Below, write your answers.

God's Path for You

When we are tested, the Book of James instructs us to "count it all joy" (James 1:2). James understood that tests serve a purpose in our spiritual development. Have you ever made a conscious effort to "count it all joy" during a painful or confusing period in your life? How did you grow spiritually from this experience? In the space below, write your thoughts.

_____

_____

_____

_____

_____

_____

_____

_____

_____

_____

_____

_____

_____

_____

Group Discussion

1. In James 1:7, the Bible tells us that God cannot bless a double-minded person. What prevents double-minded individuals from being blessed of God? How is double-mindedness corrected?

2. Oftentimes, people believe they are operating in faith, when actually they are being foolish and/or presumptuous. How can one tell the difference between faith, foolishness, and presumption?

Quote from the Bishop...

Internalizing the Word of God
is a personal experience.
There are times when I want
to talk about *Shadrach*, *Meshach* and
Abednego, but I discovered it's better
for me to talk about *your shack!*
You need the Word of God in your heart
so that your home will be blessed.
Blessings manifest wherever
His Word abides.

CHAPTER 8

SPIRITUAL COMMITMENT

This I say then,
Walk in the Spirit,
and ye shall not fulfil
the lust of the flesh.

(Galatians 5:16)

Chapter Summary

For many of us, the more we learn about the *blessing of commitment*, the more we want to live in a manner that is pleasing to God. Our desire to increase our level of commitment to the LORD grows stronger. Unfortunately, after a week or two, many of us return to our old habits. What is the problem? It was a *flesh commitment*.

Whatever you do for the Lord must be done from your spirit. When you try to do something for the Lord with your body (flesh), it is easy to get tired and sit down. A *spiritual commitment* is rooted in your desire to please God. You are able to stick with it and your spirit hangs in there because the spirit knows there is a reward for being committed.

Study Questions

1. Explain the difference between spirit and flesh.

2. Describe, in detail, how and where the flesh operates.

3. True or False: Operating in the flesh is learned behavior.

4. True or False: A carnal-minded person can submit to the Word of God.

5. According to Galatians 5:16, explain the meaning of "walking in the Spirit."

Meditation

Everything I do must give God glory. Trusting God's Word and doing things His way is sometimes a struggle, especially when I don't feel confident about the outcome of a particular situation. However, I realize that *spiritual commitment* is not about how I feel; it's about having absolute trust in an absolute God.

Reflections

Being saved and born again does not remove us from the problems and troubles that come from living in this world. However, as Christians, we should strive to handle these situations the way the Spirit, not the flesh, would have us handle them. When we walked as those who are *in the world*, if someone got under our skin, we had one type of reaction. But now that we're walking in the Spirit, we react differently.

Take a few moments to recall a situation to which you reacted in a negative manner. How would you handle this situation today? Below, write your thoughts.

_____

_____

_____

_____

_____

_____

_____

_____

_____

_____

_____

_____

God's Path for You

Many times people fall back into sin because they are trying to maintain their deliverance in the flesh. However, the flesh is not capable of maintaining your deliverance. Your deliverance is kept through the power of the Holy Spirit.

Can you think of a time when you know that it was the Holy Spirit that allowed you to resist temptation and remain in the will of God? Below, describe this experience.

_____

_____

_____

_____

_____

_____

_____

_____

_____

_____

_____

_____

_____

_____

Group Discussion

1. What does the Bible mean when it describes someone as carnal-minded (Romans, chapter 8)? How is a person's life affected when his or her self-centered, ego-driven desires are not restricted or subdued?

2. Describe a work in your ministry or church, which never could have been accomplished, without a spiritual commitment on the part of leadership and the members involved.

Quote from the Bishop...

Your spirit and flesh are at war
with each other. When you accepted
Jesus Christ as your personal Lord
and Savior, the devil lost his position.
He is no longer in control of your body,
actions, thoughts, ways, or motives.
All that you are belongs to God.

CHAPTER 9

SPIRITUAL ADULTERY

Create in me a clean heart, O God,
and renew a right, persevering,
and steadfast spirit within me.

(Psalm 51:10 The Amplified Bible)

Chapter Summary

Christians commit spiritual adultery when they say they're part of the body of Christ, yet do things that are contrary to His teachings and instructions. Because the Holy Ghost reveals all truth (John 14:26), when believers first begin to go astray, there is a check or nudge in their spirit. Unfortunately, after awhile, some get comfortable with committing spiritual adultery.

It doesn't take a long analytical process to determine if your behavior is pleasing to God. Sometimes people try to make God more complicated than He is. God is looking for someone who will do more than just "talk the talk." You must "walk the walk" and be an example of who God is. To receive *the blessing of commitment*, you must obey His commandments and allow His Word to flourish in your life.

Study Questions

1. True or False: The disobedience of one person in a church does not affect the congregation as a whole.

2. In one word, explain the biblical concept of the *house of Judah.*

3. True or False: Psalm 139 is a prayer of repentance.

4. Which prophet did the Lord send to David to confront him about his relationship with Bathsheba? What was David's response to the prophet?

5. Explain the meaning of *repentance*.

6. True or False: The adversary can do everything believers can do.

7. Using 1 Corinthians 13:1, define *charity*.

Meditation

Search me, O God, and know my heart: try me, and know my thoughts.

And see if there be any wicked way in me, and lead me in the way of everlasting. (Psalms 139:23–24)

Reflections

It is very important to take a personal inventory. An individual is in a dangerous mind-set when he cannot examine himself and ask God to see if there is any wickedness within. Too often, we're so busy knowing what's wrong with someone else, we forget about "checking" ourselves.

You must be sincere when you ask the Lord to search you because He may show you some things about yourself that you don't like. When the Lord shows some of us our ways, and it's a terrible picture, we're tempted to say, "That's not me!" However, when you ask God to search your heart, you must accept what He shows.

In prayer, ask the Lord to search your heart (motives) and your mind (thoughts). What did He show you? Below, write your answer.

_____

_____

_____

_____

_____

_____

_____

_____

_____

_____

God's Path for You

The enemy wants believers to become comfortable in their wrongdoing. He leads people to believe that no one will ever know. He wants you to forget that the Word of God says, "...and be sure your sin will find you out" (Numbers 32:23b).

If you find yourself out of position with God, you need to learn how to quickly get back in place. In Psalm 51:10, David cried out to God and asked Him to create a clean heart and renew a right spirit within him. David acknowledged his sin and repented, and pleaded for the Lord's mercy (Psalm 51:10).

Have you ever found yourself out of position with God? How did you become aware that you had strayed from God's path? What did you do to get back on track? Describe, in detail, this experience.

_____

_____

_____

_____

_____

_____

_____

_____

_____

_____

Group Discussion

1. Have you ever been involved in a church activity or program, in which the organizers were operating with the wrong motive? What was the result?

2. 1 John 4:1 tells us to *try the spirits.* How do we do this?

3. Explain the meaning of Hebrews 6:6, which says that believers who commit spiritual adultery are *crucifying Jesus afresh?*

Quote from the Bishop...

When you really make a stand and commit to God, the adversary will try to tempt you to sin and walk away from the LORD. At times like these, keep your head high and rejoice in the Word of God that says, "I can do all things through Christ which strengtheneth me" (Philippians 4:13).

CHAPTER 10

THE LUST FACTOR

For it is written,

You shall be holy,

for I am holy.

(1 Peter 1:16, The Amplified Bible)

Chapter Summary

The Greek word for holy is *hagios*, which means to be set apart—sanctified—consecrated. The Bible tells us to be holy for He is holy (1 Peter 1:16, Leviticus 11:44–45). When we are holy, we are like God and He is glorified.

The enemy, of course, does not want you to be holy—he wants you to sin. James 1:14 tells us that man (and woman) are drawn away from being like God by our *own* lust, meaning, our self-centered desires. When lust is conceived or "takes hold" it gives birth to sin; and the end result of sin is death—spiritually and physically.

My goal is for you to know and obey the Word of God so that you can be spiritually resurrected! To do this you must understand satan's tricks. Never let impulsive, selfish desires get you out of position and, consequently, make you miss the blessings God has for you. Be holy and glorify the LORD through your life!

Study Questions

1. What is the *lust factor?*

2. We enter the Lord's gates with _____, and into His courts with _____.

3. True or False: Being in a state of spiritual adultery does not affect a person's ability to praise God in the proper manner.

4. Explain how praise counteracts the negative intent of the enemy.

Meditation

I am determined to stay in position to receive the blessing of commitment and have wealth and riches released into my life. I place any thought that exalts itself against the Creator under arrest. I totally commit to His will, His way, and His Word. Lord, I lift everything to You right now. I surrender all.

Reflections

No one is exempt from being tempted. Even though you might be saved, your flesh is still vulnerable.

The devil has done his research. He's not going to tempt you with a box of cigars if he knows you can't stand the smell of them. He knows the things that are enticing to you. He knows which thoughts to plant in your mind. He knows what to do to discourage you from meditating and concentrating on the goodness of God.

What does the enemy do to entice you? When temptations occur, how do you handle them? Reflecting on your early years as a believer, has there been a change in your ability to recognize satan's tricks? Below, write your insights.

_____

_____

_____

_____

_____

_____

_____

_____

_____

_____

_____

God's Path for You

Your praise shows that you acknowledge who God is. You are reverencing Him when you tell Him, "You are my Jehovah-shalom. You are my victory and my peace. I lift my hands to You; not according to what I see, but according to what I believe."

Has there been a time in your life, in which you were determined to praise God, regardless of your circumstances? What was the outcome? Below, write about this experience.

_____

_____

_____

_____

_____

_____

_____

_____

_____

_____

_____

_____

_____

Group Discussion

1. How does one control thoughts, rationalizations, and inclinations that contradict the will, way, and Word of God?

2. Psalm 22:3 states that the Lord inhabits the praises of His people? Explain the meaning of this Scripture.

3. Discuss examples of how some believers use their freedom through Christ to justify doing whatever they please.

Quote from the Bishop...

It is not a sin to use your imagination.
God loves for you to have an imagination
and a vision of doing things to please Him.
It is sinful to imagine things that exalt
themselves against the knowledge
and the will of God.

CHAPTER 11

THE BATTLE IS THE LORD'S

Ye shall not need to fight in this battle:
set yourselves, stand ye still, and see the
salvation of the LORD with you,
O Judah and Jerusalem: fear not,
nor be dismayed; tomorrow go out against
them: for the LORD will be with you.

(2 Chronicles 20:17)

Chapter Summary

In 2 Chronicles, chapter 20, we find the Moabites, the Ammonites, and their allies preparing to attack King Jehoshaphat and the people of Judah. When the king learned about the enemy's plans, they had already entered his territory. These events occurred at a time when King Jehoshaphat had been making great strides in reforming Judah. The people were turning away from worshipping idols and false gods, and were renewing their commitment to the God of Abraham, Isaac, and Jacob.

When you make a stand for the LORD, don't be surprised if the enemy comes against you. The adversary is going to do his best to get you to back down. He wants you to hush up, sit down, and not give God perfected praise. The story of King Jehoshaphat and the people of Judah illustrates how the LORD will go to battle for His people. All we need to do is get in position, stand still, and watch Him move. *The battle is not yours— it belongs to the LORD!*

Study Questions

1. Who is the Lion of the tribe of Judah? What does the Lion symbolize?

2. True or False: Jahaziel is mentioned in the Bible on several occasions.

3. True or False: The Ammonites and Moabites came against Judah during a time when they were engaged in idolatry and were indifferent to the God of their fathers.

4. True or False: The word *Judah* in Hebrew means "prayer."

5. True or False: The army of King Jehoshaphat slaughtered the multitude that came against the people of Judah.

6. Explain, using at least four Scripture references, how Judah became the greatest of all twelve tribes of Israel.

Meditation

I restrict my tendency to fight my own battles. In times of trouble, I will seek the LORD and trust in Him. I will praise the LORD at all times, for His mercy endureth forever.

Reflections

When the enemy is at your heels, and you have nowhere to run; don't panic. This is the time to remain faithful and praise the LORD. Like a roaring, conquering lion, He will manifest Himself, and defeat the enemy for you.

Has there been a situation in your life you had to completely turn over to the Lord? How did it affect your spirituality? Below, describe in detail, this experience.

_____

_____

_____

_____

_____

_____

_____

_____

_____

_____

_____

_____

_____

_____

God's Path for You

There may be times when the LORD makes a request of us that we don't fully understand. Sometimes we are required to perform a task that goes beyond our comfort zone. The LORD might even ask us to do something that we find odd, or that could be potentially embarrassing.

Has the LORD ever instructed you to do something that was very difficult or unusual? Did you do what was asked? What did you learn from this experience? Below, write your answer.

_____

_____

_____

_____

_____

_____

_____

_____

_____

_____

_____

_____

_____

Group Discussion

1. During critical times, we cannot afford to operate in fear. When King Jehoshaphat learned of the enemy's plans, he did not panic. The king called all the men, women, and children of Judah together to seek the LORD.

   Find two examples in Scripture in which it was necessary for an individual to overcome his or her fear to accomplish the will of God. Also, find two examples where fear caused someone to be defeated by the enemy. How did these individuals differ? Analyze the chain of events that led to victory and those that led to defeat.

2. What advice would you give to someone who is afraid of the adversary?

Quote from the Bishop...

The people of Judah knew how to praise
the Lord. When Judah praised God,
He would move on their behalf. God will
always remember Judah, and He will
always remember you. He always
remembers those who praise Him.

CHAPTER 12

RUN WITH PATIENCE

WHEREFORE, seeing we also are compassed
about with so great a cloud of witnesses,
let us lay aside every weight, and the sin
which so easily beset us, and let us **run
with patience** the race that is set before us.

Looking unto Jesus the author and finisher
of our faith; who for the joy that was
set before him endured the cross,
despising the shame, and is set down
at the right hand of the throne of God.

(Hebrews 12:1–2)

Chapter Summary

Every true believer has a race and a course to run. God has a purpose and plan for your life that He wants you to fulfill. To stay in the race, you must understand that God is still God and that He is in control. When you understand that He is still God, though you may be confronted by obstacles, you won't let go of your commitment.

Any hindrance that would stop you from running your race and missing the promises of God must be put away. You cannot allow your spirit to be weighted down—it's time to obtain every blessing God has for you.

Study Questions

1. Explain the meaning of *run with patience.*

2. What did Paul and Silas do to endure their imprisonment?

3. True or False: Believers should never attack the enemy.

4. Find three biblical examples of individuals who became vulnerable to the ploys of the enemy due to a "going through" experience. In your answer, describe how the adversary used the individuals' circumstances to deceive them.

Meditation

With patience, I run the race that is set before me.

I lay aside every hindrance that would stop me from obtaining *the blessing of commitment and God's release of wealth and riches into my life.*

I keep my eyes on Jesus. He is my example. He is the originator, orchestrator, and developer of my faith.

Reflections

Hearing about Jesus is one thing; being a witness and experiencing His saving power is another. Many of us today are witnesses. We know what Jesus has done for us. We know He's a deliverer and a healer. We know Jesus will make things better. He's our Savior and keeper. He's a mind regulator. Jesus still frees people from the bondage of the enemy.

Are you a witness to the saving power of Jesus Christ? Below, write your testimony.

_____

_____

_____

_____

_____

_____

_____

_____

_____

_____

_____

_____

_____

God's Path for You

We often hear the saints talking about "going through." This is a way of saying someone is dealing with a major difficulty or problem. Something is really going wrong and if it's not one thing it's another.

To hang in there and keep on going in the through times, you need a glimpse and a vision of what's on the other side. You're not running the race because things are going well at the moment; you run because you understand there's a blessing on the other side of our through.

Describe a "going through" experience you have personally endured. How was God glorified? Below, write about this experience.

_____

_____

_____

_____

_____

_____

_____

_____

_____

_____

_____

Group Discussion

1. Why does God allow pain and suffering?

2. What are some of the signs that a person is ready for a higher level of anointing? What are some of the signs that a person is not ready?

Quote from the Bishop...

To do what God has called you to do
and go where He has called you
to go, you must be patient.

Wait patiently on God understanding that
He is working out any difficulty you may
encounter. You'll have a testimony that God
blessed you and brought you through.

CHAPTER 13

COMMIT TO A HOLY LIFE

*We know [absolutely] that anyone
born of God does not [deliberately and
knowingly] practice committing sin,
but the One Who was begotten of God
carefully watches over and protects him
[Christ's divine presence within him
preserves him against the evil],
and the wicked one does not lay hold
(get a grip) on him or touch [him].*

(1 John 5:18, The Amplified Bible)

Chapter Summary

A person who is living for God has a certain lifestyle. The Bible says that a tree is known by the fruit it bears. If you are connected to the True Vine, your life will bear the fruit of the Spirit which is love, joy, peace, longsuffering, gentleness, goodness, faith, meekness, and temperance (John 15:1–5 and Galatians 5:22–23).

Unfortunately, many Christians believe they can do whatever they want. We live among the "do what you want" generation. However, when you are living for God, you cannot do what you want and remain connected to the True Vine. You must live according to His principles and have your foundation built upon His Word.

Without a firm foundation you can easily become double-minded and get confused about how you should be living. Keep your foot on the solid foundation of God's Word so you can receive *the blessing of commitment and a release of wealth and riches into your life!*

Study Questions

1. Cite three biblical examples of a person being filled with the Holy Spirit.

2. Find three Scriptures which address speaking in "tongues." What is its purpose?

3. If someone is finding it difficult to be holy, what should he or she do?

4. True or False: The enemy never manipulates Scripture.

5. Using Titus, chapter 2, describe the character and role of older men and older women in the church.

Meditation

I delight in following God's instructions, obeying His commands, and living in a manner that pleases Him. God's Spirit gives me power to *commit to a holy life* so I can get in position to receive *the blessing of commitment. Wealth and riches will be released into my life,* and the world will know without a doubt that I am blessed!

Reflections

You must continually search yourself because there is a standard you must live by if you want to be with Christ. Everyday you need to ask yourself if your life is giving God glory.

Do you think the LORD is pleased with your lifestyle? List three behaviors you need to eliminate and three strengths you need to improve. Then reflect on how your lifestyle changes will allow you to receive *the blessing of commitment.* Below, write your answer.

_____

_____

_____

_____

_____

_____

_____

_____

_____

_____

_____

_____

_____

God's Path for You

God's standard does not have to be lowered because He will always have a remnant of believers who love and obey Him. We are precious in His sight and belong to Him. As a matter of fact, the Lord said, "And they shall be mine...in that day when I make up my jewels" (Mal. 3:17).

How has the LORD shown you that you are precious and belong to Him? Below, describe one of these experiences.

_____

_____

_____

_____

_____

_____

_____

_____

_____

_____

_____

_____

_____

_____

Group Discussion

1. Applying God's standard, describe a believer's lifestyle.

2. How does one gain greater intimacy with the LORD?

3. Instructing and providing guidance to youth and young adults is more difficult today than in the past. Why?

4. Should parents make their children go to church? What can parents do to encourage their children to participate in religious activities?

Quote from the Bishop...

Jesus is coming back for people
who have made themselves ready.
He is not coming back for people
who are contemplating *getting ready.*
He's coming for the ones who *are ready.*
You must **be ready** to meet
the soon-coming King!

CHAPTER 14

HE LOVES YOU

Fear not, little flock;
for it is your Father's good pleasure
to give you the kingdom.

(Luke 12:32)

Chapter Summary

God is moving His people into wonderful and strategic areas. Though you may be going through a storm or battle, be encouraged. God loves you so much that no weapon the enemy forms against you will be able to prosper (Isaiah 54:17). You don't have to worry, cry, or be depressed about anything because *He loves you*. You will not be defeated, destroyed, nor fail because *He loves you!*

Study Questions

1. True or False: The LORD never promised to deliver us out of all our persecutions.

2. What is *grace?*

3. True or False: Under certain circumstances, the LORD will ignore someone's sin.

4. Cite five Scriptures that describe the *love* of God.

Meditation

I will always worship God for who He is and what He will do. I realize that no matter what is going on in my life, I can find rest and comfort in His love. He will turn darkness into light and make crooked ways straight. He will create a miracle that is uniquely designed for me. God will place people in my path who are for me and remove those who are against me. He'll open some doors and close others. He's an awesome God worthy of all praise.

Reflections

Many times, we learn more about the LORD's saving grace through trials, tribulations, and very difficult times, than when everything is going well. The troubles you go through help you develop the strength to endure adversity, and allow you to personally experience God's love.

It is important for you to know, at all times, that God loves you. Describe a time in your life when you knew, without a doubt, that God loved you. Below, describe in detail, this experience.

_____

_____

_____

_____

_____

_____

_____

_____

_____

_____

_____

_____

_____

God's Path for You

The Lord rewards His children who carefully and diligently seek Him (Hebrews 11:6). He wants *wealth and riches released into your life.* It is His good pleasure to give you the Kingdom.

Are you living a life that God can reward? Do you expect to receive a *release of wealth and riches into your life?* Give each of these questions careful thought; then write your answer below.

_____

_____

_____

_____

_____

_____

_____

_____

_____

_____

_____

_____

_____

Group Discussion

Sometimes, when negative things happen to people, they become convinced that a God who *is* love would never have allowed these things to happen. How can we, as believers, encourage those who doubt God's love?

Quote from the Bishop...

Living for God will change your life.
He promises to give you *the blessing
of commitment and release wealth and
riches into your life*, but you must be
totally committed to Him. *He loves you*
and desires above all things that
you prosper and be in health,
even as your soul prospers.

(3 John 2)

PRAYER OF REPENTANCE

Father, in the precious Name of Jesus,
I magnify Your holy Name. Lord, help me
position myself to be used in Your
Kingdom. Let Your glory shine through
my life. Forgive me for my foolish ways.
I repent for spending money I did not have
and getting myself into debt. I now ask You
to transform my mind. I am going to walk
by Your Word. I will live by Your Word.
I am coming out of debt. I will no longer
be beneath. I shall be above. I will no
longer be the tail. I shall be the head.
I will no longer allow the spirit of debt to
hold me in bondage. I shall live in
prosperity. I press into You. I stand upon
Your Word. I present my body as a living
sacrifice, holy, and acceptable to You.
I totally submit to Your Word. I receive
Your promise that wealth and riches shall
be in my house. Help me to allow You
to make me rich, that I may support
Your Kingdom. In Jesus' Name. Amen.

RESEARCH PROJECTS

Your research project should include information from a minimum of three of the following sources: various translations of the Bible, biblical commentaries, concordances, and biblical dictionaries.

1. Sometimes people are under the impression that the Creator wants us to follow a "checklist" of do's and don'ts to obtain His blessings. However, the purpose of God's instructions is to help us become more like Him. Using Scripture, describe the indicators, which confirm that an individual has experienced true spiritual transformation. This essay should be two to three pages, typed, and double-spaced.

2. The Bible provides many lessons on how we should manage our finances. Find three Scripture passages, which address financial management. In your essay, include examples of biblical characters who followed the LORD's financial advice, and those who did not. Discuss the results in each case. This essay should be three to four pages, typed, and double-spaced.

3. Throughout history, the LORD has used his prophets to warn His people against idolatry. Explain the meaning of *idolatry*. How is it manifested in the Church today? Using Scripture, explain what we can learn from the prophets of old to defeat this enemy of the people of God. This essay should be four to five pages, typed, and double-spaced.

SCRIPTURE INDEX

The following index of Scriptures is taken from *The Blessing of Commitment: Releasing Wealth & Riches Into Your Life*, which this Study Guide & Journal accompanies.

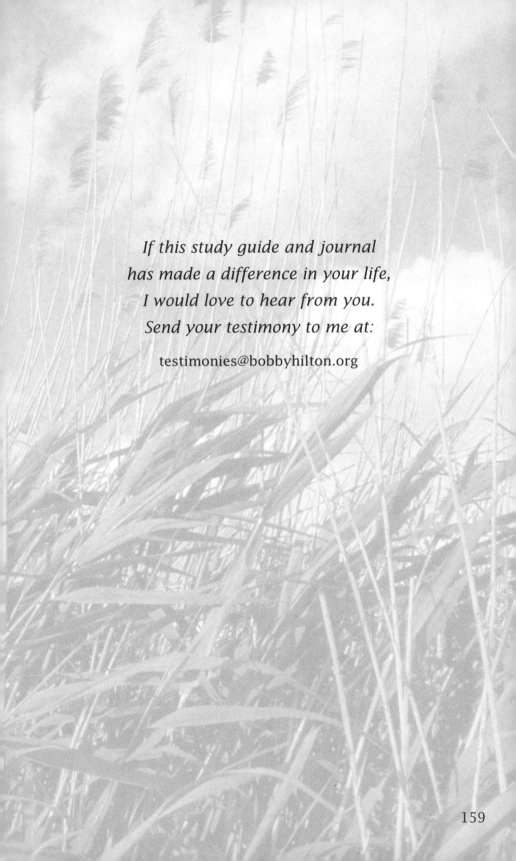

If this study guide and journal
has made a difference in your life,
I would love to hear from you.
Send your testimony to me at:

testimonies@bobbyhilton.org

ABOUT THE AUTHOR

BOBBY HILTON

There are preachers and then, there's Bobby Hilton. One who teaches while preaching, this Cincinnati-based pastor is capturing the nation's attention. Bishop Hilton has been featured on the Trinity Broadcasting Network (TBN) and on local, regional, and national television and radio shows. His television broadcast, *Taking the Word to the World™*, is viewed by people of all cultures and religious backgrounds.

Dr. Mark J. Chironna has described the bishop as "...a voice to our generation... [who] has provided us a pattern, a process, and an opportunity to commit to eternal values and see incredible results."

A minister for over twenty years, Bishop Bobby Hilton, Ph.D. is senior pastor of Word of Deliverance Ministries for the World, Inc. He is also CEO of Bishop Bobby Hilton Ministries, Inc. and Strengthening, Overcoming, Achieving, Restoring (S.O.A.R.) Development Corporation, and a chaplain with the Hamilton County Police Association. The bishop is dedicated to *Taking the Word of God to the World* via community outreach and evangelism, television, radio, books, audio and videotapes, conferences, and the Internet. He and his wife, Dr. Valda Hilton, have been married for twenty-five years and have two children.

One could say that Bobby Hilton has come a long way since 1990, when he became the pastor of a small congregation in Cincinnati. Within a few short years, the congregation has grown from 200 members to over 2200 members. With three services held every Sunday to accommodate his rapidly growing membership, Bishop Hilton is moving forward with the ministry's capital stewardship campaign, "Let Us Rise Up and Build." Two new facilities will be constructed: a 5,000-seat, state-of-the-art worship center and a 50,000 square foot family life center. The facilities are designed to meet the congregation's spiritual needs and to provide human service programs and economic solutions that facilitate the restoration and healing of individuals, families, and communities.

From the onset of his ministry, the bishop has been on a mission to tear down all walls of division—racial and denominational among others—in the body of Christ. Appreciating where God has brought him, Bishop Hilton believes he is on track to fulfill God's purpose for his life. He reflects, "Too many Christians want to stick to a predetermined format and stay within the four walls of the church. Now is the time to go beyond your comfort zone and reach out to those who are lost and in bondage." The bishop shows no hesitation in moving beyond his comfort zone. Riding on the wings of his soul-stirring teaching and electrifying preaching, Bobby Hilton is *Taking the Word of God to the World.*

Bobby Hilton
Selected Teaching Series

Audio/Videotapes	Books
Faith Zone	The Blessing of Commitment: Releasing Wealth & Riches into Your Life
I See the Lord	
Grace & Mercy	Destined for Glory: Fulfilling God's Purpose & Plan for Your Life
Spiritual Things	
I Am Persuaded	
Abiding Under the Shadow	Destined for Glory: Study Guide & Journal For Fulfilling God's Purpose & Plan for Your Life
Anointed	
Embracing the Spirit of Abundance	The Blessing of Commitment: Study Guide & Journal For Releasing Wealth & Riches Into Your Life
Discerning the Times	

SCHOLASTIC SERIES TEST

Name _____
(Please print your name as it should appear on your Certificate of Completion.)

Organization _____

Address _____

City _____ State _____ Zip _____

Telephone (_____) _____

E-mail _____

---

1. Using three Scripture references, explain the meaning of "transformed by the renewing of our minds."

2. What factors have contributed to the acceptance of debt as a "part of life" in today's culture?

3. When the children of Israel left Egypt, they had doubts about God's willingness to fulfill His promises. What caused this doubt? Were they able to overcome it?

4. Why does the LORD deliver His people from debt?

5. True or False: Money is the root of all evil.

6. Deuteronomy, chapter 28, describes the blessings God has for His people. List five blessings noted in this chapter. What must one do to receive these blessings?

7. How does one move from confessing God's promises that have been declared in the spirit realm, to manifestation in the physical realm?

8. What is God's plan concerning the wealth of the sinner?

9. Hosea 4:6 says, "My people are destroyed for lack of knowledge." What is God's position towards those who reject knowledge?

10. Isaiah 10:27 tells us, "…and the yoke shall be destroyed because of the anointing." Explain how this aspect of the anointing applies to the burden of debt.

11. Why are some people afraid of money?

12. What are God's instructions for people who borrow from their tithes (Leviticus 27:31)?

13. How does the Bible describe someone who does not pay his or her tithes and offerings? What are the consequences for disobeying God's instructions concerning this matter?

14. It is our Father's good _____ to give us the _____ (Luke 12:32).

15. If you remain thankful and pay your vows unto the Most High, in the day of trouble you can call upon Him and He will _____ you.

16. Explain the meaning of deliverance.

17. List five tools the enemy uses to keep people in bondage.

18. True or False: Confession is an essential step for obtaining deliverance.

19. In the fight against the enemy, what are three weapons believers should possess and use?

20. In Genesis 12:2–3, what did God promise Abram (Abraham)?

21. Explain justification through faith.

22. When Abraham left Egypt, he was very rich in cattle, silver, and gold. How did he accumulate these possessions?

23. How long were the children of Israel held in bondage by the Egyptians:

    a) 200 years b) 300 years c) over 400 years

24. The wealth of the sinner is laid up for the _____.

25. After giving the children of Israel wealth and freeing them from the Egyptians, what did God ask of them?

26. Explain God's principle of increase.

27. At the beginning of the Book of Exodus, the children of Israel were slaves and had nothing. In Exodus 36:5, they have much more than enough to do God's work. Spiritually, how did this dramatic change come about?

28. What was the adversary trying to prove to God about Job?

29. The Psalms written by King David often tell of praising the LORD regardless of the circumstances. Find three Psalms that reflect a posture of praise to the Creator at all times. What conclusion does David reach in each of these Psalms?

30. Describe two aspects of our inner being that ignite a release of wealth and riches into our lives (Psalm 112).

31. True or False: Holiness refers to a denomination.

32. True or False: A lifestyle of transgression is easier than a lifestyle of holiness.

33. Explain, using the principles discussed in this chapter, the meaning of being *humble*.

34. Why did God bless Abraham?

35. Citing the New Testament, find an example of God freeing His people from debt.

36. True or False: One can know God without knowing His Word.

37. John 6:63 says, "It is the spirit that quickeneth; the flesh profiteth nothing...." Explain the meaning of this verse.

38. Using practical, real life examples, explain the difference between knowledge and wisdom.

39. True or False: Joy is derived from external circumstances and situations.

40. True or False: God gives wisdom only to people who are spiritually mature.

41. Explain, using at least three Scripture references, the biblical meaning of faith.

42. Explain the difference between spirit and flesh.

43. Describe, in detail, how and where the flesh operates.

44. True or False: Operating in the flesh is learned behavior.

45. True or False: A carnal-minded person can submit to the Word of God.

46. According to Galatians 5:16, explain the meaning of "walking in the Spirit."

47. True or False: The disobedience of one person in a church does not affect the congregation as a whole.

48. In one word, explain the biblical concept of the house of Judah.

49. True or False: Psalm 139 is a prayer of repentance.

50. Which prophet did the Lord send to David to confront him about his relationship with Bathsheba? What was David's response to the prophet?

51. Explain the meaning of repentance.

52. True or False: The adversary can do everything believers can do.

53. Using 1 Corinthians 13:1, define charity.

54. What is the lust factor?

55. We enter the Lord's gates with _____, and into His courts with _____.

56. True or False: Being in a state of spiritual adultery does not affect a person's ability to praise God in the proper manner.

57. Explain how praise counteracts the negative intent of the enemy.

58. Who is the Lion of the tribe of Judah? What does the lion symbolize?

59. True or False: Jahaziel is mentioned in the Bible on several occasions.

60. True or False: The Ammonites and Moabites came against Judah during a time when they were engaged in idolatry and were indifferent to the God of their fathers.

61. True or False: The word Judah in Hebrew means "prayer."

62. True or False: The army of King Jehoshaphat slaughtered the multitude that came against the people of Judah.

63. Explain, using at least four Scripture references, how Judah became the greatest of all twelve tribes of Israel.

64. Explain the meaning of run with patience.

65. What did Paul and Silas do to endure their imprisonment?

66. True or False: Believers should never attack the enemy.

67. Find three biblical examples of individuals who became vulnerable to the ploys of the enemy due to a "going through" experience. In your answer, describe how the adversary used the individuals' circumstances to deceive them.

68. Cite three biblical examples of a person being filled with the Holy Spirit.

69. Find three Scriptures which address speaking in "tongues." What is its purpose?

70. If someone is finding it difficult to be holy, what should he or she do?

71. True or False: The enemy never manipulates Scripture.

72. Using Titus, chapter 2, describe the character and role of older men and older women in the church.

73. True or False: The LORD never promised to deliver us out of all our persecutions.

74. What is grace?

75. True or False: Under certain circumstances, the LORD will ignore someone's sin.

76. Cite five Scriptures that describe the love of God.

TEST SCORING
AND CERTIFICATE
OF COMPLETION

Please retain a copy of your test for your records. We will grade your test and mail your score to you. Certificates of Completion will be issued to individuals who have a correct score of 70% to 100% on the test.

This test can also be downloaded from my website: **www.bobbyhilton.org**. Please print your name and contact information on the first page of the test. Completed tests can be faxed to (513) 742-3458 or mailed to:

BBHM
690 Northland Blvd.
Forest Park, OH 45240
ATTN: Publications Department

LIFE–CHANGING
BOOK

Throughout the text, Hilton clearly unfolds the reasons we can and should achieve our God-given destiny, encouraging as he empowers. This well-written book is an easy read. It is inspiring and scripturally sound.

—Teresa Hairston,
Publisher/CEO
Gospel Today magazine

Destined for Glory provides a biblically based foundation for understanding God's purpose and plan for our lives. When individuals understand their destination, they are more apt to endure the struggles that are an inherent part of the journey. Bishop Bobby Hilton motivates and encourages believers to pursue their God-ordained purpose. This book demonstrates how even during times when the situation seems hopeless, God will step in and see us through to our destiny.

<table>
<tr><td>Destined
for Glory</td><td>Destined for Glory
Study Guide & Journal</td></tr>
<tr><td>Bishop Bobby Hilton</td><td>Bishop Bobby Hilton</td></tr>
<tr><td>ISBN: 1-930766-28-9</td><td>ISBN: 1-930766-37-8</td></tr>
<tr><td>Trade:192 pages</td><td>Concealed Wirebound:144 pages</td></tr>
<tr><td>Price: $12.99</td><td>Price: $14.99</td></tr>
</table>

Available at Your Local Christian Bookstore
Visit our website at: bobbyhilton.org

LIFE–CHANGING

AUDIO/VIDEO SERIES

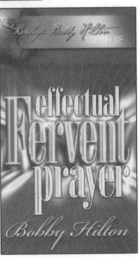

Discerning the Times	**Anointed**
Bishop Bobby Hilton	*Bishop Bobby Hilton*
4-Tape Audio ISBN: 1-930766-26-2 – $22	4-Tape Audio ISBN: 1-930766-19-X – $22
2-Tape Video ISBN: 1-930766-27-0 – $35	2-Tape Video ISBN: 1-930766-20-3 – $35
Spiritual Things	**Effectual Fervent Prayer**
Bishop Bobby Hilton	*Bishop Bobby Hilton*
4-Tape Audio ISBN: 1-930766-13-0 – $22	4-Tape Audio ISBN: 1-930766-26-2 – $22
2-Tape Video ISBN: 1-930766-14-9 – $35	2-Tape Video ISBN: 1-930766-27-0 – $35

ANOTHER *Life-Changing* BOOK

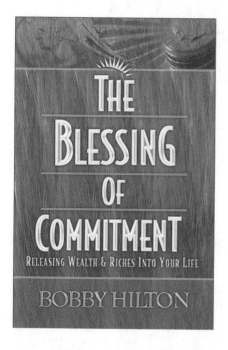

If you're expecting God to do great things through you and for you, this book is a must-read.
—Dr. Creflo A. Dollar

Bishop Bobby Hilton, a voice to our generation has provided us a pattern, a process, and an opportunity to commit to eternal values and see incredible results. This book will create a pathway to genuine blessing.
—Dr. Mark J. Chironna

Bishop Hilton has effectively isolated the time-tested principles that guarantee success and equip readers with the tools to experience God's best in life.
—Dr. Myles Munroe

Bishop Bobby Hilton provides sound biblical principles and practical applications at a time when many teachings on prosperity resemble secular, get-rich-quick schemes. Bishop Hilton shows readers the true pathway to obtaining the wealth and riches God has declared for the Kingdom.

The Blessing of Commitment
Bishop Bobby Hilton
ISBN: 1-930766-25-4
Trade:182 pages
Price: $12.99

The Blessing of Commitment Study Guide & Journal
Bishop Bobby Hilton
ISBN: 1-930766-38-6
Concealed Wirebound:176 pages
Price: $14.99